A Refugee's Story

**Valerie Sinason and Sheila Hollins
with Hina Gillani and Elizabeth Laird
illustrated by Mike Nicholson**

Beyond Words

London

4

28

ISBN 978-1-78458-149-7

British Library Cataloguing-in-Publication Data

A catalogue record for this book is available from the British Library.

Printed by Royal British Legion Industries, Leatherhead.

Books Beyond Words is a Charitable Incorporated Organisation (no. 1183942).

Further information about the Books Beyond Words series can be obtained from Beyond Words' website: www.booksbeyondwords.co.uk.

Contents

	page
A possible storyline	42
A poem by Hina Gillani	46
What does it mean to be a refugee?	47
Disabled refugees	49
What can communities do to help?	50
Useful resources	51
Related titles	53
Authors, Artist and Contributors	55
Acknowledgments	57
Dedication	58
Beyond Words: publications and e-learning	59
How to read this book	60

A possible storyline

Do make up your own story from the pictures first. The following words are some other people's ideas about the story. There is no right or wrong story.

1. Ali is at home with his family. He takes their photo.

2. Ali plays football with his little brother, Omar.

3. The war comes to Ali's town. There are bombs and bullets. Homes are destroyed and people are hurt and killed.

4. Ali's father is killed. Their family is heartbroken.

5. Ali's mother and sister pack a bag with food. Everyone is quiet and sad. Outside, the war gets worse.

6. Ali and Omar cannot stay any longer. The war is too dangerous. Their mother, sister and grandfather cannot make the journey, so they have to say goodbye. They don't know when or whether they will see each other again.

7. Lots of people from the towns and villages are leaving to find safety. Ali and Omar join the crowd.

8. The journey is long and hard. Ali and Omar have no shelter. They are scared and worn out.

9. On the road, Ali asks another man to cut his hair. Maybe it will help him feel more normal? But there is nothing normal about this journey.

10. Ali and Omar reach a camp for refugees. There are so many people here. "I want to go home," says Omar. "I know, but we have to keep going. We will be safe soon," says Ali.

11. Ali paid a man to take him and Omar across the sea. The man lied to him. He doesn't let Omar in the boat with Ali.

12. The sea is rough and there are too many people in the boat. Ali is scared they will sink.

13. The boat lands on a beach where there are lots of people in uniforms. Ali is tired, wet and cold. A man offers Ali a towel.

14. They take Ali and the other people from the boat to a secure place. Ali feels very alone. He keeps thinking about Omar.

15. Ali is driven in a van through a strange new town. "Where are we going? What is going to happen to me?" he thinks.

16. A different official meets Ali when the van arrives. She asks him questions in her language, but Ali doesn't understand.

17. An interpreter translates what the officer says for Ali. She makes sure that Ali understands and helps him to communicate with the official.

18. Ali explains what happened with Omar. "I need to find my brother," he tells her.

19. Ali is in a hostel with lots of other men. He still doesn't know where Omar is. He misses his whole family.

20. The other men in the hostel chat, eat and drink together. It's very noisy, and Ali feels even more lonely.

21. A man introduces himself to Ali. He offers him some food.

22. Ali doesn't like the strange food very much. His mother's cooking is much better.

23. Ali walks around the town. It is busy and noisy. He doesn't know anyone.

24. Ali stops at a café. This is the food he likes!

25. Ali talks to the man at the counter. His name is Mr Hassan.

26. Mr Hassan sits with Ali as he eats his lunch. "This is my family," Ali tells him. "Things were good before the war."

27. Ali sees a poster about football on the wall.

28. "The local football club needs more players," says Mr Hassan. "Maybe you could join the team."

29. Mr Hassan takes Ali to football practice. The other players welcome him and give him a shirt.

30. Ali plays football with his new teammates. He has a great time.

31. At night, Ali dreams about his family cheering him on at a football match. It's a good dream.

32. A social worker arrives at the hostel to see Ali. "My name is John," he says. He shows Ali his work ID.

33. John says, "We have found your brother, Omar." Ali can't believe it.

34. Omar is outside with John. They wait for someone to let them in.

35. Ali answers the door! The brothers are reunited.

36. Ali phones their mother. It is so good to hear each other's voices.

37. Ali and Omar call their mother using video. They can see their sister and grandfather too. Their family is far apart but they are all safe.

38. Ali and Omar play football together, like they did back home.

39. Ali, Omar and their friends share a meal together at Mr Hassan's café.

A Poem

by Hina Gillani

Words of love, words of expressions.

My voice your voice sewn together in a patch of quilt.

To keep you warm, to keep me warm at the times of
cold and darkness.

To keep you alive and to keep me and Us alive.

Words to wisdom, words to strive.

Words to live, words to die.

What does it mean to be a refugee?

Refugees and asylum seekers sometimes call themselves survivors, but before that they are people – ordinary people who had to leave their own homes and their own countries because something happened that made their lives unsafe. The reasons people leave are many, including war, famine, climate emergency, political or religious unrest or being in a minority.

Sometimes the journeys people are forced to take are unsafe too. They may have risked their lives travelling in small boats without life jackets. They may have spent all their savings on the journey, or they may have been cheated out of their savings and possessions by someone falsely promising a safe passage. They may have spent time living in camps that are unhealthy and overcrowded. Refugees are not the same as migrants who are people leaving their own country in search of a better life.

Refugees come from many countries in Europe, Africa, Asia and Latin America. For example, there are lots of refugees from Syria, Somalia and Afghanistan. Television and newspapers often show rows of white tents in refugee camps with people queuing for food and water. But most refugees are living in villages, towns and cities where they are working hard to rebuild their lives. At the time of going to press, refugees from Ukraine represent the largest number of displaced people on the move.

The United Nations High Commissioner for Refugees says that sheltering and supporting people fleeing bombs, bullets, torture and rape is not an act of charity, it is a legal and moral obligation prescribed both by international law and by our common humanity.

Nevertheless, many counties differentiate between people seeking asylum who have arrived by legal and illegal routes. All have suffered. The pictures in this book do not make a judgement on these policies. Instead, they have been carefully designed to reflect real experiences, although there are many different experiences that have not been included, such as gender and age. Each person has their own story to tell.

Disabled refugees

Millions of people become refugees every year and it's likely 1 in 7 are disabled children or adults. Sadly, when families flee from war or political unrest, some older and disabled family members will be left behind. For those who do make the journey, they can find it even harder to access the help they need.

When refugees arrive in a new country, few local organisations working with disabled people will have any experience of working with refugees and their particular trauma. And organisations working with refugees have little experience of working with disabled people or refugee families with disabled children.

Few interpreters and a lack of knowledge or information about disability rights and possible support mean that people's needs are not met if services don't work together. Standard language courses, for example, may not be accessible for people with learning disabilities. Word-free stories, however, can be particularly helpful for disabled people in refugee communities because they are not language dependent.

What can communities do to help?

Maybe some of your neighbours are refugees? They may need help to begin with, for example to learn to speak English, to furnish their new homes and clothe their families.

Welcoming your new neighbours and getting to know them is the most important thing you can do. They may be worrying about the family members they left behind and missing them. Asking them about their family and their country will help you to understand, and will show them that you care.

In the UK, there is a government website (www.gov.uk/help-refugees) that can link you to local support provided by councils and voluntary organisations. Often, they need help to provide:

- housing
- fostering
- donations of goods such as clothes and toys.

Perhaps you could pass on this story to be given with donations of goods to new refugees arriving in your area.

Refugees may need help to speak a new language or to get work, but most importantly they need friendship.

Useful resources

Organisations, services and initiatives in the UK

Refugee Council
This organisation provides support and advice to refugees and asylum seekers, and campaigns to bring about positive change for refugees in the UK.
www.refugeecouncil.org.uk

Help refugees who have come to the UK
The Home Office has lots of information about the different ways you can help refugees coming to the UK, including donations, sponsorship, volunteering and offering employment.
www.gov.uk/help-refugees

City of Sanctuary UK
A network of groups across the UK working to build welcoming communities for people seeking sanctuary. The network comprises community groups, councils, libraries and schools. Their website offers a range of resource packs for organisations wanting to best support people seeking sanctuary within their sector.
www.cityofsanctuary.org

Refugee Week
Managed by Counterpoints Arts, this UK-wide festival celebrates the contributions, creativity and resilience of refugees and people seeking sanctuary. Anyone can get involved by taking part in an event or organising one. The annual festival is timed to coincide with World Refugee Day on 20 June.
www.refugeeweek.org.uk

The Migration Museum

This free museum in London explores how the movement of people to and from Britain has shaped who we are – as individuals, as communities, and as a nation. The museum regularly hosts new exhibitions and offers education visits for schools as well as an online resource bank.
www.migrationmuseum.org

Helen Bamber Foundation

Support for refugees and asylum seekers who are survivors of trafficking and torture through specialist services: therapy; medical advice; legal protection; counter-trafficking support; housing and welfare advice; and more.
www.helenbamber.org

Digital resources

Asylum seeker and refugee mental health information

The Royal College of Psychiatrists has developed resources for health and social care professionals working with people affected by global conflicts.
www.rcpsych.ac.uk/international/humanitarian-resources

Supporting refugees with intellectual disabilities

Inclusion Europe members have shared best practice for supporting refugees with intellectual disabilities.
www.inclusion-europe.eu/refugees-with-disabilities-in-poland-moldova-romania-czechia

Safe Place app

A meditation app for refugee children and young people who may be experiencing PTSD and anxiety.
www.ustwo.com/work/safe-place/

Related titles in the Books Beyond Words series

When the War Came (2022) illustrated by Lucyna Talejko-Kwiatkowska. A short story that provides a starting point for conversations about the war in Ukraine.

Jenny Speaks Out (2015, 3rd edition) by Sheila Hollins and Valerie Sinason, illustrated by Beth Webb. Jenny feels unsettled when she moves into a new home in the community. Her carer and friends sensitively help Jenny to unravel her painful past as a victim of sexual abuse, and begin a slow but positive healing process.

Bob Tells All (2015, 2nd edition) by Sheila Hollins and Valerie Sinason, illustrated by Beth Webb. Bob has moved to a group home, but his erratic behaviour and terrifying nightmares unsettle the other people living there. A social worker sensitively helps Bob unravel his painful past as a victim of sexual abuse, and begin a slow, but positive, healing process.

I Can Get Through It (2009, 2nd edition) by Sheila Hollins, Christiana Horrocks and Valerie Sinason, illustrated by Lisa Kopper. This book tells the story of a woman whose life is suddenly disturbed by an act of abuse. It shows how with the help of friends and counselling, the memory of the abuse slowly fades.

Ron's Feeling Blue (2011, 2nd edition) by Sheila Hollins, Roger Banks and Jenny Curran, illustrated by Beth Webb. Ron is depressed and has no interest in doing things. With the help of his GP and family he begins to feel better.

Sonia's Feeling Sad (2011) by Sheila Hollins and Roger Banks, illustrated by Lisa Kopper. Sonia is feeling so sad that she shuts herself off from her family and friends. She agrees to see a counsellor and gradually begins to feel better.

When Somebody Dies (2014, 2nd edition) by Sheila Hollins, Sandra Dowling and Noëlle Blackman, illustrated by Catherine Brighton. Shows how a man and a woman are helped by regular bereavement counselling sessions, and the comfort and companionship shown by friends, to learn to feel less sad and to cope with life better and better as time passes.

When Mum Died (2014, 4th edition) by Sheila Hollins, and Lester Sireling, illustrated by Beth Webb. The story of a family dealing with the death of a parent told through pictures in a simple, honest and moving way. This book shows a burial.

When Dad Died (2014, 4th edition) by Sheila Hollins and Lester Sireling, illustrated by Beth Webb. A partner book to *When Mum Died*, showing a family dealing with the loss of a father. This book shows a cremation.

Accessing health services

Many stories in the Books Beyond Words series address health topics, and can help people understand about accessing health care services in a new country and what to expect from appointments.

Authors, Artist and Contributors

Valerie Sinason is the grandchild of refugees and her thinking for this story was also in their honour. A widely published poet, writer, and psychoanalyst she is President of the Institute for Psychotherapy and Disability. She was Founder Director and now Patron of the Clinic for Dissociative Studies and was given a lifetime achievement award at the International Society for the Study of Trauma and Dissociation.

Sheila Hollins chairs the charity Beyond Words, which she was inspired to found with artist Beth Webb and with her autistic son, Nigel. She commissions new titles and works ceaselessly to get these word-free stories into the hands of people who find pictures easier than words. She is an independent member of the House of Lords and Emeritus Professor of Psychiatry of Disability at St George's, University of London, as well as being a past President of the Royal College of Psychiatrists and the British Medical Association.

Hina Gillani is a poet from Pakistan. She is also a member of St Augustine's Centre and Sisters United, a user-led group in Calderdale for women from all backgrounds, many of whom have experience of asylum/immigration systems.

Elizabeth Laird is a British writer of children's fiction and travel. She is also known for the large body of folktales which she collected from the regions of Ethiopia. Her stories "Welcome to Nowhere" and "A House Without Walls" are inspired by the time she spent in Jordan meeting young people and their families living in refugee camps. Her books have been translated into at least twenty languages. Elizabeth's website is: www.elizabethlaird.co.uk

Mike Nicholson has illustrated for numerous clients, including Penguin Books, Weekend Guardian, Amnesty International and the BBC. As a storyboard artist he has worked with many comedy writers, directors and performers, including Reeves and Mortimer, Armando Iannucci and Matt Berry. His autobiographical zines have been collected widely, including by The British Library, Tate Zine Library and Wellcome Library. See: *@ensixteen_editions* and www.ensixteeneditions.blogspot.com

Acknowledgments

We are thankful to everyone who has contributed to the development of this story, including Mark Linington, Osama Sharkia, Bridget Chapman, Zoran Bozovic, Renos Papadopoulos, Katie Clarke and Alicia Wood.

We also wish to thank all the people who read earlier drafts of the picture story, including Sisters United; Stories of Hope and Home, Birmingham; Rochdale Borough Council, Early Help & Schools; Exeter College ESOL students; Uniting Friends: Charmaine, Abi and Catherine supported by Michelle; Your Voice Advocacy, Swansea; the ESOL E1/E2 conversation group at MHTS; Susie Chidzik; MacIntyre i4t: Sharon, Lisa, Kim, Alan, Christine, Andrew and Louise with Carole and Rachel; Mid Kent book club: Dawn, Paul, Danny, Margaret, James, Mark, Angela, Kim and Sue; Deal book club: Katie, Helen, Mandy, Will, Paul, Julie, Marc, Mark, Taimi and Anne; The Pulse Book Group Sittingbourne, Service User Group at Therapeutic Support Services facilitated by Jane Williams at Bryn Y Neuadd Hospital Betsi Cadwaladr University Health Board, Della Shenton, Pothiti (Toula) Kitromilidi, Nikolaos Axiotis and Ahmad Maihanwal.

We are grateful to Valerie Sinason, The 3Ts Charitable Trust and Colyer-Fergusson Charitable Trust for their generous financial support of this resource.

Dedication

In honour of my Ukrainian Buba
Who emerged from exile
Wise, wounded and illiterate
My Polish Nanna
Whose trauma and learning disability
Made her love shine through even brighter
My fine courageous parents
Who rose up British from their jigsaw nests
And in loving memory of my son
Who died of cancer of the pancreas
All my dear dead my exiles my refugees

Sometimes our ancestors
Come after us and carry us with them
And sometimes they come before

May we all find refuge in them
May they find refuge in us
Together
In our Heartlands

- Valerie Sinason

Beyond Words: publications and e-learning

Books Beyond Words are stories for anyone who finds pictures easier than words. There are more than 60 word-free (and therefore non-language dependent) stories in the Books Beyond Words series, all co-created with our readership. Our stories empower people to make their voices heard and to be actively involved in the choices and events that affect their lives.

- A complete list of all Beyond Words publications, including print and eBook versions, can be found on our website:
  www.booksbeyondwords.co.uk

- E-learning modules about using Books Beyond Words will also be useful for some people. You can find out more about e-learning and how to subscribe on our website:
  www.booksbeyondwords.co.uk/elearning

- Books Beyond Words are used in many different environments, including health care settings, schools and colleges and community book clubs. Various resource packages are available for professionals wishing to incorporate the stories into their practice. See our website or contact us for more information:
  admin@booksbeyondwords.co.uk

- Video clips showing our books being read are also on our website and YouTube channel:
  www.youtube.com/booksbeyondwords

How to read this book

This is a story for anyone who finds pictures easier to understand than words. It is not necessary to be able to read any words at all.

1. Start at the beginning and read the story in each picture. Encourage the reader to turn the pages themselves.

2. Whether you are reading the book with one person or with a group, encourage them to tell the story in their own words. You will discover what each person thinks is happening, what they already know, and how they feel. You may think something different is happening in the pictures yourself, but that doesn't matter. Their interpretation tells you about their life experience.

3. Some people will follow the story without any problems. If a picture is more difficult, it can help to prompt with open questions, gradually going deeper into the meaning, for example:
    *   I wonder who that is?
    *   I wonder what is happening?
    *   What is he or she doing now?
    *   I wonder how he or she is feeling?
    *   Have you felt like that? Has it happened to you/ your friend/ your family?

4. You don't have to read the whole story in one sitting. Allow people time to follow the pictures at their own pace. Stay longer with any pictures they are drawn to.